# Beyond

# 9-5:

A Young Entrepreneur's Guide to Building

Residual Income

## Table of Contents:

- Budgeting for business investments.

6. Chapter 5: Essential Tools and Resources
- Overview of tools for business planning, financial management, and productivity.
- Leveraging online resources and communities.

***Part III: Pathways to Residual Income***
7. Chapter 6: Digital Products and Services
- Creating and selling ebooks, courses, and webinars.
- Subscription models and membership sites.

8. Chapter 7: E-Commerce and Dropshipping
- Setting up an online store.
- The fundamentals of dropshipping.

9. Chapter 8: Content Creation and Monetization
- Blogging, YouTube, and podcasting.
- Affiliate marketing and advertising revenue.

10. Chapter 9: Investing for Future Income
- Basics of stock market investing.
- Real estate investments and REITs.

**Part IV: Scaling and Beyond**

11. Chapter 10: Automating Your Income Streams

- Tools and strategies for automation.

- Outsourcing and building a team.


12. Chapter 11: Scaling Your Business

- When and how to expand.

- Diversification of income streams.


**Part V: Building a Legacy**

13. Chapter 12: Networking and Community Building

- Importance of building a strong network.

- Leveraging social media and online communities.


14. Chapter 13: Using AI

- The advancement of technology and AI as a tool

- The big secret!


This outline is designed to take you on a comprehensive journey, equipping them with the knowledge, tools, and inspiration they need to break free from the 9-5 and build a life of entrepreneurial success and financial freedom. Each part builds upon the last, ensuring all readers develop a solid understanding before moving on to more complex topics.

## Chapter 1: Understanding Residual Income

Welcome to the first step of your journey beyond the conventional 9-5 grind. This chapter lays the groundwork for everything you need to know about residual income—a key concept that will enable you to build financial freedom and live life on your terms. By understanding what residual income is, you'll be better equipped to identify opportunities and make informed decisions as you build your path to entrepreneurial success.

*The Essence of Residual Income*

Residual income, often interchanged with passive income, is money you continue to earn without the need for continuous, active work. Unlike a traditional 9-5 job, where you trade hours for dollars, residual income generates ongoing earnings from work done once. It's the cornerstone of financial independence, allowing you to grow your wealth even when you're not working.

*Examples of Residual Income*

**Royalties from books or music**: Earnings received every time someone purchases your book or streams your song.

**Rental income**: Money earned from renting out property.

**Dividend-paying stocks**: Regular payments received for owning a company's stock.

**Online courses or digital products**: Sales generated long after the initial product creation and launch.

## The Power of Residual Income

Understanding the power of residual income is crucial for aspiring entrepreneurs. It offers several life-changing benefits:

### Financial Freedom

Residual income can provide a safety net that allows you to cover your living expenses without relying on a traditional job. It's about creating a future where your income doesn't depend on your daily efforts.

### Time Freedom

With residual income streams, you reclaim your time. You can choose to work when and how you want, giving you the freedom to pursue your passions, travel, or spend time with loved ones.

### Scalability

There's a limit to how much you can earn in a traditional job, constrained by hours in the day and salary ceilings. Residual income opportunities, on the other hand, can be scaled, potentially leading to unlimited earnings.

*Building Blocks of Residual Income*

To successfully build residual income, you need to understand its building blocks:

*Initial Effort and Investment*

Creating a source of residual income often requires upfront effort, time, or capital. Whether it's writing a book, purchasing a rental property, or starting a business, initial investment is key.

*Value Creation*

For your income stream to be sustainable, it must offer value to others. Whether it's providing knowledge through a course or offering accommodation through rental property, value drives income.

*Maintenance and Growth*

While the goal is to minimize active involvement, some maintenance is necessary to ensure your income streams continue to grow and don't diminish over time.

Residual income isn't just a dream reserved for the few; it's an achievable goal for anyone willing to put in the initial effort. As you embark on this journey, remember that the path to financial independence begins with understanding and leveraging the power of residual income. In the coming chapters, we'll dive deeper into how you can identify opportunities, lay the foundations for your residual income streams, and ultimately, build a life beyond the 9-5.

---

## Chapter 2: Mindset Shifts for Success

Transitioning from the security of a 9-5 job to the world of entrepreneurship and residual income requires more than just knowledge and skills—it demands a significant shift in mindset. This chapter delves into the essential mental adjustments aspiring entrepreneurs must make to thrive in an environment where success is self-determined and failure is part of the learning process.

*Embracing an Entrepreneurial Mindset*

The foundation of any successful entrepreneurial journey is the mindset. Shifting your mindset from that of an employee to an entrepreneur is crucial.

*From Security to Uncertainty*

**Accepting Risk**: Understand that risk is a part of the entrepreneurial process. Learn to assess and take calculated risks.
**Tip**: Start small to manage risk without jeopardizing your financial security.

*From Directive to Self-Driven*

**Cultivating Self-Motivation**: Without a boss to set deadlines, self-motivation becomes key.
**Strategy**: Set clear, achievable goals. Use milestones to celebrate progress, keeping motivation high.

*From Fixed Income to Variable Rewards*

**Adapting to Income Fluctuations**: Prepare mentally and financially for fluctuating incomes.
**Advice**: Maintain a financial buffer to smooth out income variances, reducing stress and allowing focus on growth.

*Overcoming Fear and Embracing Failure*

Fear of failure is one of the biggest obstacles for new entrepreneurs. Learning to reframe failure as a learning opportunity is a game-changer.

*Failing Forward*

**Redefining Failure**: View failure as feedback, not a setback. Each failure teaches you what doesn't work, bringing you closer to what does.

**Tip**: Keep a journal of lessons learned from each failure to improve decision-making over time.

*The Power of Resilience*

**Building Resilience**: Cultivate the ability to bounce back from setbacks stronger than before.
**Strategy**: Develop a support network of mentors and peers. Sharing challenges and solutions can provide new perspectives and emotional support.

*Continuous Learning and Adaptability*

The landscape of entrepreneurship and residual income is ever-changing. Staying informed and adaptable ensures long-term success.

*Lifelong Learning*

**Embrace Curiosity**: Stay open to new ideas, technologies, and methods.
**Advice**: Allocate time each week for learning. Online courses, books, and podcasts are great resources.

*Staying Flexible*

**Adapting to Change**: Be prepared to pivot your strategies in response to market shifts or feedback.

**Tip**: Regularly review your business model and income streams. Be willing to adjust or diversify as needed.

*Cultivating a Network*

Success in entrepreneurship is seldom a solo journey. Building a robust network can provide invaluable support, advice, and opportunities.

*The Value of Mentors*

**Seeking Guidance**: Find mentors who have achieved what you aspire to. Their experience can help you avoid common pitfalls.

**Strategy**: Attend industry events and participate in online communities to connect with potential mentors.

*Peer Support*

**Building a Community**: Surround yourself with fellow entrepreneurs. Peer support can motivate you and provide practical advice.

**Tip**: Join or create mastermind groups focused on residual income and entrepreneurship.

Adopting an entrepreneurial mindset is the first critical step on your journey beyond the 9-5. This chapter has explored key mindset shifts, from embracing uncertainty and risk to cultivating resilience and a thirst for continuous learning. Remember, the path to building residual income and achieving financial freedom is both a mental and practical endeavor. With the right mindset, you are well-equipped to navigate this journey successfully.

---

**Chapter 3: Identifying Your Niche**

Dedicated to one of the greatest salespeople this world has ever been graced with: Zig Ziglar!

*"Success comes when opportunity meets preparation,"* Zig Ziglar once said, and nowhere is this truer than in the entrepreneurial quest for residual income. Identifying your niche is not just about spotting an opportunity; it's about aligning that opportunity with your unique set of skills, passions, and the preparation to excel. This chapter is dedicated to helping you find that alignment, that sweet spot where you can not only succeed but thrive.

*The Significance of Finding Your Niche*

Your niche is your personal claim in the vast world of business. It's where your product or service meets a specific need in a way that no one else can. Many professionals and CEOs believe in the power of individuality and the strength that comes from knowing your unique value proposition.

*Why Niche Down?*

**Focused Expertise**: Specializing allows you to become an expert in a specific area, providing better value to your customers.

**Less Competition**: A well-defined niche means less competition and a clearer path to becoming a market leader.

**Increased Profitability**: Customers are willing to pay a premium for specialized expertise and products.

**STRATEGY:**

#### Step 1: Inventory Your Passions and Skills

"Success occurs when opportunity meets preparation." Start by listing your passions and skills. What do you love doing? What are you good at? Your niche often lies at the intersection.

#### Step 2: Identify Problems You Can Solve

"You can have everything in life you want if you will just help enough other people get what they want." Look for problems in your areas of interest that you are uniquely qualified to solve.

#### Step 3: Research and Validate Market Demand

"Lack of direction, not lack of time, is the problem. We all have twenty-four-hour days." Use your time wisely to research if there's a demand for the solution you're offering. Validate your ideas through market research, surveys, and pilot programs.

## Crafting Your Unique Value Proposition (UVP)

Your UVP is a clear statement that describes the benefit of your offer, how you solve your customer's needs, and what distinguishes you from the competition. Ziglar's philosophy teaches us to focus on the value we bring to others.

### Elements of a Strong UVP

- **Clarity**: Be clear about what you offer and to whom.
- **Specificity**: Be specific about the benefits and how you deliver them.
- **Uniqueness**: Highlight what makes you different.

"Ziglar-Inspired" Strategies for Developing Your UVP*

**Serve, Don't Sell**: Focus on how your product or service will enrich your customers' lives.
**Be a Solution, Not a Choice**: Position yourself as the solution to a problem, not just another option among many.

## Market Analysis and Positioning

"Your attitude, not your aptitude, will determine your altitude."
Zig Ziglar
Approach your market analysis with a positive attitude and a belief that you will find your place within it.

### Understanding Your Audience

Know who your audience is, what they need, what they value, and how they prefer to receive information. This understanding is crucial for effective communication and marketing.

### Analyzing Your Competitors

"Remember that failure is an event, not a person." Study your competitors not to fear failure but to learn from their journey and find gaps you can fill.

Continuing with Chapter 3 on identifying your niche, let's dive deeper using the impactful delivery styles associated with notable success coaches, focusing on goal setting and prioritization, massive action and presence, and mental toughness and self-accountability.

## Setting Clear, Achievable Goals

Success begins with a clear picture of your destination. Without precise goals, your efforts can become scattered and ineffective. To carve out your niche, start with a vision that excites you—a vision so compelling that it draws you towards it.

### Visioning Your Niche

Imagine your niche not just as a sector of the market, but as the very arena where your passions and skills meet the world's needs. What does it look like? Who are you helping? How does it feel to be the go-to person in this space?

### Goal Mapping

Break down this vision into actionable goals. These should be specific, measurable, attainable, relevant, and time-bound (SMART). Each goal becomes a stepping stone on your path to dominance within your niche.

## Embracing Massive Action

The difference between those who dream and those who achieve is the scale of their action. To not just enter but own your niche requires action that's not just consistent but expansive. Think of your efforts as ripples spreading across a pond; aim to make waves instead.

### Saturate the Space

Be everywhere. Use every platform at your disposal to share your message, your knowledge, and your passion. This isn't about spreading yourself thin; it's about creating a presence so strong that your name becomes synonymous with your niche.

### Over-Delivering Value

Before asking for a single dollar, flood the market with value. Free resources, actionable advice, insights from your journey— these not only build your reputation but also create a community of followers who trust and respect you.

## Developing Mental Fortitude

The path is fraught with obstacles. It's your response to these challenges that defines your journey. Developing a mindset of resilience and unwavering determination is non-negotiable.

### The Comfort in Discomfort

Seek out challenges. Embrace discomfort as a tool for growth. Each obstacle overcome is a layer of toughness added to your resolve. Remember, the most significant growth often happens outside your comfort zone.

### Radical Accountability

Hold yourself to a standard so high that others are inspired by it. This means taking full responsibility for your actions, your decisions, and most importantly, your results. Look in the mirror every day and ask yourself, "Did I do everything I could to move closer to my goals?"

Identifying your niche and making a mark within it is a blend of strategic planning, Herculean effort, and the mental toughness to persevere through setbacks. It's about setting clear, compelling goals, taking massive, targeted action, and cultivating a mindset that not only expects obstacles but embraces them as opportunities for growth.

Your niche is out there, waiting for you to claim it. But it requires more than just identification—it demands dedication, action, and a relentless pursuit of excellence. With every step taken, every piece of value provided, and every challenge faced head-on, you're not just finding your place in the market; you're defining it.

## Chapter 4: Financial Planning and Management for the Entrepreneurial Spirit

In the entrepreneurial journey, mastering the art of financial planning and management is not just a skill—it's the very backbone of your success. This chapter delves into the strategic and disciplined approach to finance that sets the foundation for sustainable growth and the ultimate achievement of financial freedom.

### *The Blueprint of Financial Mastery*

Understanding the numbers behind your business is critical. But this isn't just about keeping a ledger of income and expenses. It's about crafting a financial blueprint that aligns with your entrepreneurial vision, propelling you toward your goals with precision and clarity.

### *Vision-Driven Budgeting*

Start with your end goal in sight. What financial milestones must you hit to achieve your entrepreneurial dreams? Reverse-engineer your path to these milestones, setting clear budgetary guidelines that serve not just as constraints but as stepping stones toward your success.

*Capital Allocation Strategy*

Every dollar in your business serves a purpose. It's a soldier in your army marching towards conquest. Allocate your capital with strategic intent—prioritizing investments in areas with the highest return potential, whether it be marketing, product development, or talent acquisition.

*Navigating the Financial Waters with Agility*

The financial landscape is as tumultuous as the sea—conditions can change rapidly, and storms can appear on the horizon with little warning. Your ability to navigate these waters with agility and foresight determines not just your survival but your ability to thrive.

*Building Your Financial Forecast*

A robust financial forecast is your compass. It guides your journey, helping you anticipate changes and adjust your sails accordingly. This forecast should be grounded in reality but flexible enough to adapt to unforeseen challenges and opportunities.

*The Art of Cash Flow Management*

Cash flow is the lifeblood of your business. Managing it effectively means ensuring that the timing of cash inflows matches, or ideally exceeds, your outflows. Mastering cash flow management allows you to seize opportunities and weather downturns with confidence.

*Creating a Safety Net*

Entrepreneurship is inherently risky. A safety net is not just a buffer—it's a strategic asset that enables you to take calculated risks with confidence, knowing that you have the resilience to bounce back from setbacks.

*Emergency Fund Essentials*

An emergency fund is your financial shock absorber. Aim to set aside a reserve of at least six months' worth of operating expenses. This fund ensures that you can continue essential operations and pursue growth initiatives, even in lean times.

*Diversification: Beyond Just a Financial Portfolio*

Diversification in entrepreneurship extends beyond your investment portfolio. It applies to your income streams, your customer base, and even your supplier relationships. Diversifying reduces your vulnerability to single points of failure, ensuring your business's longevity.

*Leveraging Financial Data for Strategic Decisions*

Data is power. Financial data, analyzed with keen insight, can unveil patterns, trends, and opportunities that might otherwise remain hidden. It's not just about tracking metrics—it's about interpreting them to inform strategic decisions.

*Key Performance Indicators (KPIs)*

Identify the KPIs that matter most to your business. These might include customer acquisition cost, lifetime value, gross margin, and more. Monitoring these KPIs closely allows you to optimize operations and maximize profitability.

*The Feedback Loop of Financial Review*

Institute a regular process for financial review—not just an annual exercise but a dynamic, ongoing feedback loop. This enables you to course-correct in real-time, refining your strategies and operations to enhance financial performance continually.

---

Financial planning and management for the entrepreneur is an art form—a blend of vision, discipline, agility, and strategic foresight. It requires a deep understanding of both the micro and macroeconomic factors that influence your business. But more than anything, it demands a commitment to continuous learning and adaptation.

As you turn the pages of this chapter and apply its principles, remember that your financial strategy is not just about numbers. It's about crafting a story of success, resilience, and eventual triumph. In the grand narrative of your entrepreneurial journey, let financial mastery be the theme that underpins every chapter of your success.

## Chapter 5: Harnessing Essential Tools and Resources for Entrepreneurial Success

In this era of rapid technological advancement and abundant information, leveraging the right tools and resources is not merely an advantage—it's a necessity for the modern entrepreneur. Chapter 5 is a deep dive into the ecosystem of digital and physical resources designed to streamline operations, amplify your message, and accelerate your path to success.

*Building Your Entrepreneurial Toolkit*

The journey from idea to execution is fraught with challenges, yet equipped with the right tools, these obstacles transform into stepping stones. Here, we explore the indispensable tools that should inhabit every entrepreneur's toolkit, aiding in everything from project management to customer engagement.

*Project Management Platforms*

Efficiency and organization are the bedrock of any successful venture. Project management tools like Asana, Trello, or Monday.com enable you to streamline workflows, collaborate seamlessly with your team, and keep track of deadlines and milestones.

- **Action Point**: Choose a platform that aligns with your team's size and complexity of projects. Familiarize yourself with its features through tutorials and leverage templates to hit the ground running.

*Financial Management Software*

Understanding the numbers behind your business is crucial. Financial software solutions like QuickBooks, FreshBooks, or Xero offer a comprehensive overview of your financial health, from invoicing and payroll to expense tracking and tax preparation.

- **Action Point**: Integrate your financial software with your bank accounts and payment systems for real-time monitoring and analysis. Regularly review financial reports to make informed decisions.

*Digital Marketing Tools*

In the digital age, visibility is currency. Tools such as Google Analytics, Hootsuite, or Mailchimp provide invaluable insights into your marketing campaigns, allowing you to refine your strategies, understand your audience, and enhance engagement.

- **Action Point**: Set clear goals for each campaign and regularly monitor performance metrics to identify what works and what needs adjustment. Embrace A/B testing to optimize your messaging and design.

*Expanding Your Knowledge Base*

The only constant in entrepreneurship is change. Staying informed and continuously learning is not just beneficial—it's essential for staying ahead. Below are key resources to fuel your growth and keep you at the cutting edge of your industry.

*Online Learning Platforms*

Platforms like Coursera, Udemy, or LinkedIn Learning offer courses on virtually every subject imaginable, from digital marketing to blockchain technology. These resources can help you acquire new skills or deepen existing ones.

- **Action Point**: Dedicate time each week to professional development. Choose courses that not only align with your current needs but also anticipate future industry trends.

*Networking Groups and Forums*

Communities such as Reddit's r/Entrepreneur, LinkedIn groups, or local Meetup events can provide support, advice, and opportunities for collaboration. Sharing challenges and solutions with peers can offer new perspectives and inspire innovative solutions.

- **Action Point**: Engage actively in these communities. Offer your insight where you can and don't hesitate to ask for advice. The value of networking is reciprocal.

*Industry Publications and Blogs*

Staying abreast of industry trends and news is crucial. Subscribing to publications like Harvard Business Review, Forbes, or niche blogs in your field can provide you with a steady stream of insights and innovations.

- **Action Point**: Implement a daily reading habit. Use tools like Feedly to aggregate content from your favorite sources for easy access.

---------------------------------------------------------------------------------

The entrepreneurial journey is a blend of vision, tenacity, and strategic resource utilization. In this digital age, the tools and resources at your disposal are more powerful and accessible than ever before. By harnessing these assets effectively, you can optimize your operations, engage with your audience on a deeper level, and navigate your path to success with confidence.

As we close this chapter, remember that the most powerful tool at your disposal is your mindset. With a commitment to continuous learning, adaptability, and strategic action, you can leverage these tools and resources not just to succeed, but to thrive in the ever-evolving landscape of entrepreneurship.

## Chapter 6: Digital Products and Services: The Pathway to Passive Income

In the digital age, the creation and sale of digital products and services stand as a beacon for entrepreneurs looking to establish streams of residual income. Chapter 6 delves into the world of digital entrepreneurship, providing a blueprint for developing, marketing, and scaling digital products and services that can significantly contribute to your financial independence.

### Unleashing the Power of Digital Products

Digital products possess a unique advantage—they require no physical inventory, have low overhead costs, and offer the potential for infinite scalability. From ebooks to online courses, software to stock photography, the digital realm is ripe with opportunities for entrepreneurs willing to explore its depths.

### Identifying Your Digital Product Niche

Your journey begins with identifying a niche that aligns with your expertise, passion, and market demand. Conduct thorough market research to uncover gaps in the current offerings and areas where your knowledge can address a specific need or problem.

- **Action Point**: Use tools like Google Trends, forums, and social media to gauge interest in topics related to your expertise. Look for questions that frequently arise and areas where there seems to be a lack of comprehensive resources.

*Developing Your First Digital Product*

The development of your digital product should focus on quality and value. Whether it's an ebook, course, or app, your product must solve a problem or fulfill a need for your target audience.

- **Action Point**: Start small with a minimum viable product (MVP). Gather feedback from early users to refine and improve before investing in more complex features or content.

*Monetizing Digital Services*

Digital services offer another avenue for generating residual income, with options ranging from consulting and coaching to design services and beyond. The key to success lies in packaging your expertise in a way that delivers value and convenience to your clients.

*Setting Up Subscription Models*

Subscription-based models provide a consistent revenue stream, transforming one-time transactions into long-term relationships. This model works well for services that offer ongoing value, such as coaching programs, premium content memberships, or software as a service (SaaS).

- **Action Point**: Clearly define what subscribers will receive and ensure that the value you provide exceeds the cost of the subscription. Regularly update and refresh your offerings to keep the subscription valuable.

*Automating Service Delivery*

Automation is a cornerstone of passive income. For digital services, this could mean setting up automated booking systems, using email marketing for lead nurturing, or creating self-serve platforms where clients can access your services or content at their convenience.

- **Action Point**: Identify aspects of your service that require repetitive tasks and explore software solutions that can automate these processes. This not only saves you time but also enhances the customer experience.

*Marketing Your Digital Products and Services*

With a digital product or service in hand, your focus must shift to marketing—getting your offering in front of the right eyes. Effective marketing strategies can catapult your digital goods from obscurity to must-have resources.

*Building an Online Presence*

A robust online presence establishes your authority and builds trust with your potential customers. Utilize content marketing, SEO, and social media to share valuable insights related to your niche, drawing people to your digital storefront.

- **Action Point**: Create a content calendar to regularly publish helpful blog posts, videos, or social media content that aligns with your product's value proposition. Use SEO best practices to increase your visibility in search engine results.

*Leveraging Email Marketing*

Email marketing remains one of the most effective ways to nurture leads and convert them into customers. By building an email list, you have a direct line to engage with potential and existing customers, offering them valuable content, product updates, and exclusive deals.

- **Action Point**: Offer a freebie related to your product (e.g., a free chapter of your ebook, a trial of your software, or a mini-course) in exchange for email sign-ups. Use this list to build a relationship with your audience by providing continuous value.

The digital landscape offers unprecedented opportunities for entrepreneurs to build and scale residual income streams through digital products and services. By focusing on areas where you can deliver unique value, leveraging automation and subscription models, and employing strategic marketing, you can establish a profitable and sustainable digital business.

As we wrap up this chapter, remember that the journey to successful digital entrepreneurship is iterative. It requires ongoing learning, adaptation, and innovation. With persistence and a commitment to delivering value, your digital offerings can become a cornerstone of your entrepreneurial success and a significant contributor to your financial freedom.

## Chapter 7: E-Commerce and Dropshipping: Launching Your Online Store

In the realm of entrepreneurial ventures, e-commerce stands out as a powerful gateway to financial independence, with dropshipping serving as a particularly accessible entry point for many aspiring entrepreneurs. This chapter explores the intricacies of starting and scaling an e-commerce business, emphasizing the dropshipping model as a means to minimize upfront investment while maximizing potential returns.

*Foundations of E-Commerce Success*

E-commerce offers a platform for entrepreneurs to reach a global audience with their products. However, the key to thriving in this digital marketplace lies not just in what you sell, but how you sell it.

*Choosing Your E-Commerce Niche*

Selecting a niche is about finding a balance between passion and profitability. Research market trends, consumer pain points, and competitor analysis to identify niches with high demand and low saturation.

- **Action Point**: Utilize tools like Google Keyword Planner, Trend Hunter, and social media analytics to identify trending products and untapped niches.

*Building Your E-Commerce Platform*

Your online store is your digital storefront. Whether you choose a platform like Shopify, WooCommerce, or Magento, the goal is to create a user-friendly, visually appealing site that converts visitors into customers.

- **Action Point**: Prioritize ease of navigation, high-quality product images, and clear call-to-actions (CTAs) when designing your store. Consider hiring a professional if design and development are not your strengths.

*Dropshipping: A Low-Risk Entry into E-Commerce*

Dropshipping allows you to sell products without holding inventory, significantly reducing the barrier to entry. By partnering with suppliers who fulfill orders directly to customers, you can focus on marketing and customer service.

*The Mechanics of Dropshipping*

Understanding the dropshipping model is crucial for setting up your business for success. Establishing relationships with reliable suppliers and setting up an efficient order processing system are foundational steps.

- **Action Point**: Use directories like AliExpress, SaleHoo, or Doba to find reputable suppliers. Test order processes to ensure quality and delivery times meet your standards.

*Profit Margins and Pricing Strategies*

While dropshipping offers lower upfront costs, profit margins can be thinner. Developing a pricing strategy that covers your costs while remaining competitive is essential.

- **Action Point**: Conduct thorough competitor analysis to understand pricing dynamics in your niche. Consider leveraging value-added content or exclusive offers to justify higher prices.

*Marketing Your E-Commerce Store*

With the foundations in place, the success of your e-commerce business hinges on your ability to attract and retain customers.

Effective marketing strategies can propel your store from obscurity to market presence.

*SEO and Content Marketing*

Search engine optimization (SEO) and content marketing are long-term strategies that build organic visibility and establish your brand as an authority in your niche.

- **Action Point**: Optimize product descriptions, blog content, and site metadata for relevant keywords. Create informative and engaging content that addresses your target audience's needs and interests.

*Leveraging Social Media and Influencer Partnerships*

Social media platforms and influencer partnerships can drive traffic and sales by tapping into established audiences and leveraging social proof.

- **Action Point**: Identify influencers within your niche who align with your brand values. Collaborate on sponsored content or affiliate marketing campaigns to reach a wider audience.

*Scaling Your E-Commerce Business*

As your e-commerce store grows, scaling becomes the next challenge. Exploring new marketing channels, expanding your product line, and optimizing your operations are key strategies for growth.

*Diversification and Expansion*

Expanding into new markets or adding complementary products to your offering can drive additional revenue streams and reduce dependency on a single product or market.

- **Action Point**: Regularly review sales data and customer feedback to identify opportunities for expansion. Consider international markets if your supply chain supports it.

*Customer Retention and LTV Optimization*

Acquiring a new customer is often more expensive than retaining an existing one. Implement strategies to increase customer lifetime value (LTV), such as loyalty programs, email marketing, and personalized offers.

- **Action Point**: Use email marketing to keep your brand top of mind with regular updates, exclusive offers, and valuable content. Implement a loyalty program to reward repeat customers.

------------------------------------------------------------------------

Launching and scaling an e-commerce and dropshipping business requires a blend of strategic planning, relentless marketing, and continuous optimization. By understanding the fundamentals of e-commerce, leveraging the dropshipping model to minimize risk, and employing effective marketing and growth strategies, you can build a profitable online business that stands the test of time.

Remember, the journey of e-commerce entrepreneurship is one of constant learning and adaptation. Stay informed, stay agile, and let your passion for your products and your customers guide you to success.

## Chapter 8: Content Creation and Monetization: Building Your Brand

In the digital age, content is not just king—it's the currency of the realm. Chapter 8 dives into the world of content creation and monetization, a pivotal strategy for entrepreneurs looking to establish their brand, engage with their audience, and create additional streams of residual income.

*The Power of Content Creation*

Creating compelling, valuable content is at the heart of digital marketing and brand building. Whether it's through blogging, video production, podcasting, or social media, content creation offers a platform to share your expertise, insights, and stories, connecting with your audience on a deeper level.

*Identifying Your Content Niche*

Just as with your business, your content should focus on a specific niche. This niche should align with your brand's expertise and your audience's interests, addressing their questions, challenges, and needs.

- **Action Point**: Use tools like BuzzSumo, AnswerThePublic, or Google Keyword Planner to research topics that resonate within your niche. Look for gaps in the existing content that you can fill.

*Developing a Content Strategy*

A strategic approach ensures your content efforts contribute to your business goals. Define the purpose of your content, whether it's to educate, entertain, or inspire. Plan your content types, channels, and posting schedule to maintain consistency and engagement.

- **Action Point**: Create a content calendar outlining topics, formats, and publication dates. This will help you stay organized and consistent with your content production.

*Monetizing Your Content*

With a loyal audience and a robust catalog of content, monetization becomes a viable next step. There are multiple ways to generate income from your content, from direct sales to affiliate marketing.

*Affiliate Marketing*

Promote products or services relevant to your niche through affiliate programs. You earn a commission for each sale made through your referral links.

- **Action Point**: Join affiliate networks related to your niche. Choose products you genuinely believe in to promote to your audience, maintaining trust and authenticity.

*Sponsored Content*

Collaborate with brands to create content that promotes their products or services. These partnerships can be lucrative but choose collaborations that align with your brand values and resonate with your audience.

- **Action Point**: Pitch to brands with a proposal that highlights your audience demographics, engagement rates, and how your content aligns with their marketing goals.

*Selling Digital Products or Services*

Your content can serve as a marketing tool for your own digital products or services, such as ebooks, courses, consulting, or merchandise.

- **Action Point**: Leverage your content to build interest and demand for your products. Use calls-to-action (CTAs) to direct your audience to your products or services.

*Expanding Your Reach*

To maximize the impact and monetization potential of your content, expanding your reach is essential. Utilize multiple channels and strategies to attract a broader audience.

*SEO for Content*

Optimize your content for search engines to improve visibility and attract organic traffic. Research and include relevant keywords, create quality backlinks, and ensure your website is search engine friendly.

- **Action Point**: Conduct keyword research for each piece of content you create. Include these keywords naturally in your titles, headings, and throughout the content.

Social media platforms can amplify your content's reach, while email marketing allows you to communicate directly with your audience, building deeper relationships.

- **Action Point**: Share your content across your social media profiles, encouraging shares and engagement. Use email newsletters to notify subscribers of new content and exclusive offers.

Content creation and monetization offer a dynamic pathway to build your brand, engage with your audience, and open up new revenue streams. By producing valuable, relevant content and leveraging various monetization strategies, you can establish a strong online presence and turn your content into a profitable asset.

Remember, the journey of content creation is ongoing. It requires patience, creativity, and adaptability. Stay true to your brand, listen to your audience, and continually refine your approach to content and monetization. With dedication and strategy, your content can become a cornerstone of your entrepreneurial success.

## Chapter 9: Investing for Future Income: Smart Strategies for Entrepreneurs

For entrepreneurs, the goal isn't just to generate income but to build wealth that sustains and grows over time. Chapter 9 explores the essential world of investing, offering insights and strategies for entrepreneurs looking to diversify their income streams and secure their financial future.

*Understanding the Investment Landscape*

Before diving into specific investment strategies, it's crucial to grasp the broader landscape. Investments can range from the stock market and real estate to more niche areas like startups and cryptocurrencies. Each carries its own risk and potential reward profile.

*Assessing Your Risk Tolerance*

Your investment strategy should align with your risk tolerance. This tolerance is influenced by your financial goals, timeline, and comfort with volatility.

- **Action Point**: Conduct a self-assessment or consult with a financial advisor to understand your risk tolerance. Use this as a guide to allocate your investment portfolio.

*Setting Investment Goals*

Clear, achievable goals form the backbone of a successful investment strategy. Whether it's retirement, purchasing property, or funding future entrepreneurial ventures, your goals will dictate your investment choices.

- **Action Point**: Define your short-term and long-term financial goals. Consider how much capital you'll need and the timeline for each goal.

*Diversifying Your Investment Portfolio*

Diversification is a key principle of investing, helping to mitigate risk by spreading investments across different asset classes.

*Stocks and Bonds*

Stocks offer a share in the ownership of a company, while bonds are essentially loans made to corporations or governments.

Both can provide income through dividends (stocks) or interest payments (bonds), though they come with different risk levels.

- **Action Point**: Start with a mix of stocks and bonds that fits your risk tolerance. Consider index funds or ETFs for broad market exposure.

*Real Estate*

Real estate investing can provide both rental income and capital appreciation. Options range from direct property investment to real estate investment trusts (REITs), which offer more liquidity and lower entry points.

- **Action Point**: Research local real estate markets for direct investment opportunities, or explore REITs for a more hands-off approach.

*Alternative Investments*

Venture into startups, cryptocurrencies, or commodities as part of your portfolio for potentially higher returns, acknowledging the increased risk.

- **Action Point**: Allocate a small portion of your portfolio to alternative investments. Stay informed and cautious, particularly with highly volatile assets like cryptocurrencies.

*Smart Investing Practices*

Adopting smart investing practices is crucial for long-term success and wealth building.

*Continuous Learning*

Stay informed about market trends, new investment opportunities, and financial literacy. The more you know, the better equipped you'll be to make informed decisions.

- **Action Point**: Dedicate time each week to financial education through books, podcasts, and reputable financial news sources.

*Reinvesting Dividends and Returns*

Reinvesting dividends and returns can compound your wealth over time, turning modest initial investments into significant assets.

- **Action Point**: Opt for dividend reinvestment plans (DRIPs) where available, and consider automatically reinvesting returns from bonds or REITs.

*Seeking Professional Advice*

While it's important to educate yourself, seeking advice from financial advisors can provide tailored investment strategies based on your personal financial situation and goals.

- **Action Point**: Consult with a financial advisor to develop or review your investment plan, especially for complex situations or significant investment decisions.

Investing is a powerful tool for entrepreneurs to diversify their income and build long-term wealth. By understanding the investment landscape, assessing your risk tolerance, setting clear goals, and adopting a diversified investment strategy, you can position yourself for financial success. Remember, the key to effective investing is a balance between informed decision-making and risk management, coupled with a long-term perspective. Stay committed to your financial education and growth, and let your investments fuel your entrepreneurial journey and personal wealth aspirations.

## Chapter 10: Automating Your Income Streams: Leveraging Technology for Passive Wealth

In the modern economy, the ability to generate income passively has become increasingly accessible, thanks to advancements in technology. Chapter 10 delves into the realm of automating your income streams, a crucial step for entrepreneurs seeking to maximize their financial efficiency and create lasting wealth with minimal ongoing effort.

*The Essence of Automation in Business*

Automation involves using technology to perform tasks with little to no human intervention, turning active income endeavors into passive or semi-passive income streams. It's about working smarter, not harder, allowing you to focus on strategic growth while maintaining or even increasing your income.

*Identifying Automation Opportunities*

Start by reviewing your current income streams and business operations to identify processes that can be automated. This could range from sales processes and customer service to marketing and financial management.

- **Action Point**: List all repetitive and time-consuming tasks within your operations. Research tools and software that can automate these tasks, such as CRM systems, email marketing software, and accounting tools.

*Automating Digital Products and E-Commerce*

For entrepreneurs in the digital product and e-commerce spaces, automation can significantly enhance efficiency and profitability.

*Digital Product Sales*

Automate the sales process for digital products like e-books, courses, and software through online platforms that handle transactions, delivery, and even marketing.

- **Action Point**: Utilize platforms like Gumroad, Teachable, or Shopify, which offer built-in automation for selling digital products. Set up automated email sequences for post-purchase engagement and upselling.

*Dropshipping and E-Commerce Automation*

In a dropshipping model, automation can cover everything from order processing to inventory management and customer communication.

- **Action Point**: Use dropshipping tools like Oberlo with Shopify to automate product imports, order fulfillment, and tracking updates. Implement chatbots or automated customer service solutions to handle common inquiries.

*Leveraging Affiliate Marketing*

Affiliate marketing can become a significant passive income stream when combined with content automation strategies.

*Content and SEO Automation*

Automate content creation and SEO optimization to drive traffic to affiliate products. Tools and AI can help create content, while plugins can optimize SEO automatically.

- **Action Point**: Explore AI writing assistants for content creation. Use SEO tools like Yoast SEO for WordPress to automate on-page SEO tasks.

*Email Marketing Automation*

Set up automated email marketing campaigns to promote affiliate products to your audience at optimal times.

- **Action Point**: Use email marketing platforms like Mailchimp or ConvertKit to create automated sequences that nurture leads and promote affiliate offers based on subscriber behavior.

*Investing and Financial Automation*

Smart investment strategies supported by automation can contribute significantly to your passive income portfolio.

*Robo-Advisors for Investment*

Robo-advisors use algorithms to manage your investments based on your risk tolerance and goals, offering a hands-off approach to growing your wealth.

- **Action Point**: Consider investing with robo-advisors like Betterment or Wealthfront. Set up automatic transfers from your bank account to invest a fixed amount monthly.

*Automating Savings and Debt Payments*

Use apps and banking tools to automate savings and manage debt, ensuring you're always building your net worth.

- **Action Point**: Set up automatic savings plans into high-yield savings accounts or investment accounts. Use automated payment setups to ensure you're consistently paying down debts.

Automation is a powerful ally in the quest for financial freedom, allowing entrepreneurs to scale their income without a proportional increase in effort. By identifying areas within your business and personal finances where automation can be applied, you can free up valuable time, reduce stress, and focus on what truly matters—growing your business and enjoying the fruits of your labor.

The journey to automated income is iterative and requires continuous optimization. Stay informed about new technologies and strategies that can enhance your automation efforts. With the right tools and a forward-thinking approach, you can transform your income streams into a well-oiled machine that generates wealth on autopilot.

## Chapter 11: Scaling Your Business: Strategies for Growth and Expansion

After establishing a solid foundation and automating key processes, the next logical step in the entrepreneurial journey is scaling your business. Scaling involves strategically growing your business in a sustainable way that increases revenue without a corresponding increase in costs. This chapter explores effective strategies for scaling your business, focusing on expansion, efficiency, and maximizing impact.

### Understanding the Foundations of Scaling

Before diving into specific strategies, it's crucial to understand what makes a business ready to scale. Scalability means your business can handle growth without being hampered by its structure or available resources.

### Assessing Scalability

Evaluate your current business model, operations, and market demand to determine if you're ready to scale. Consider if your product or service can be offered to a broader market or if there are new markets you can enter.

- **Action Point**: Conduct a scalability audit. Review your operations, customer feedback, and market conditions to identify potential barriers to scaling and opportunities for growth.

*Strategic Expansion Methods*

Growth can be achieved through various means, from market expansion and diversification to product line extensions and strategic partnerships.

*Market Expansion*

Expanding into new geographical areas or targeting new demographics within existing markets can open up new revenue streams.

- **Action Point**: Research potential new markets, considering cultural, economic, and regulatory factors. Start with small tests to gauge demand before fully committing resources.

*Diversification*

Introducing new products or services that complement your existing offerings can attract new customers and increase revenue from current customers.

- **Action Point**: Identify gaps in your product line or new needs of your customers. Develop or source new offerings that align with your brand and meet these needs.

*Leveraging Technology for Growth*

Technology can play a crucial role in scaling your business, from improving operational efficiency to opening up new channels for marketing and sales.

*E-Commerce and Digital Marketing*

Utilize online platforms to reach a global audience. Digital marketing strategies, such as SEO, social media marketing, and email marketing, can drive traffic and sales at scale.

- **Action Point**: Invest in a robust e-commerce platform. Scale your digital marketing efforts by focusing on high-ROI activities and automating where possible.

*Data Analytics and Customer Insights*

Data analytics can offer insights into customer behavior, market trends, and operational efficiency, informing strategic decisions for growth.

- **Action Point**: Implement analytics tools across your website, social media, and sales platforms. Regularly review data to identify trends and opportunities for optimization.

*Building a Scalable Team*

As your business grows, so does the need for a team that can support and drive that growth. Building a scalable team involves hiring for potential, fostering a culture of innovation, and leveraging outsourced talent.

*Hiring and Development*

Hire individuals not just for current roles but for their potential to grow with the company. Invest in training and development to build a skilled, adaptable team.

- **Action Point**: Develop clear career paths within your organization. Offer professional development opportunities to encourage growth and retention.

*Outsourcing and Delegation*

Outsourcing can be an effective way to manage costs while accessing specialized skills. Delegating responsibilities frees up your time to focus on strategic growth.

- **Action Point**: Identify non-core activities that can be outsourced. Use platforms like Upwork or Fiverr to find freelancers or agencies that can take over these tasks.

*Financial Management for Scaling*

Effective financial management is critical to successful scaling. This includes securing funding for growth, managing cash flow, and ensuring profitability at scale.

*Funding Growth*

Explore funding options to fuel your expansion, from venture capital and angel investors to bank loans and crowdfunding.

- **Action Point**: Prepare a solid business plan and pitch deck if seeking external funding. Clearly articulate your growth strategy and how the funds will be used.

*Cash Flow Management*

Maintain a keen focus on cash flow management as you scale. Growing businesses often require significant investment before realizing increased revenue.

- **Action Point**: Develop cash flow forecasts and regularly review your financials. Implement strategies to minimize cash flow gaps, such as adjusting payment terms or leveraging lines of credit.

-------------------------------------------------------------------------------

Scaling your business is an exciting phase that requires careful planning, strategic investment, and a focus on efficiency. By expanding thoughtfully, leveraging technology, building a scalable team, and managing your finances effectively, you can grow your business sustainably and maximize your impact in the market. Remember, scaling is not just about growing bigger—it's about growing smarter, ensuring that as your business expands, your foundations remain solid and your vision clear.

**Chapter 12: Harnessing the Power of AI: Transforming Your Business with Artificial Intelligence**

The advent of Artificial Intelligence (AI) has revolutionized the way businesses operate, offering unprecedented opportunities for efficiency, personalization, and innovation. This chapter explores how entrepreneurs can harness the power of AI to transform their businesses, streamline operations, enhance customer experiences, and stay competitive in the rapidly evolving digital landscape.

## Understanding AI and Its Potential

Before delving into specific applications, it's crucial to understand what AI is and its vast potential for businesses. AI refers to computer systems designed to mimic human intelligence, performing tasks from simple data analysis to more complex problem-solving and decision-making.

### The Scope of AI in Business

AI's applications in business are vast, ranging from automating routine tasks to providing deep insights into customer behavior and market trends. It can improve decision-making, enhance productivity, and open new avenues for innovation and growth.

- **Action Point**: Identify areas within your business that could benefit from automation or enhanced data analysis. This could include customer service, marketing, sales, or operations.

## Integrating AI into Your Business Operations

Leveraging AI can lead to significant improvements in operational efficiency and effectiveness. Here are key areas where AI can make a difference:

### Automating Administrative Tasks

AI-powered tools can automate repetitive administrative tasks such as scheduling, email management, and data entry, freeing up time for more strategic activities.

- **Action Point**: Implement AI-driven software like virtual assistants or automated scheduling tools to handle routine administrative tasks.

### Enhancing Customer Service

AI chatbots and virtual assistants can provide 24/7 customer service, handling inquiries, and resolving issues promptly, improving customer satisfaction and loyalty.

- **Action Point**: Deploy AI chatbots on your website and social media channels to offer instant support to customers. Train these systems regularly to improve their accuracy and helpfulness.

## Leveraging AI for Marketing and Sales

AI can transform your marketing and sales efforts, offering personalized experiences to customers and insightful data to businesses.

### Personalized Marketing

AI algorithms can analyze customer data to deliver highly targeted marketing messages and product recommendations, significantly improving engagement and conversion rates.

- **Action Point**: Use AI-powered marketing platforms to segment your audience and tailor your marketing campaigns based on customer behavior and preferences.

### Predictive Sales Analytics

AI can predict future sales trends based on historical data, enabling businesses to make informed decisions about inventory, pricing, and sales strategies.

- **Action Point**: Implement AI-driven analytics tools to forecast sales trends. Use these insights to adjust your sales strategies and inventory management practices proactively.

## Innovating with AI

AI not only optimizes existing processes but also opens up new possibilities for innovation and product development.

### Product and Service Innovation

AI can help businesses identify new opportunities for products or services and enhance existing offerings with intelligent features.

- **Action Point**: Explore how AI can add value to your products or services. Consider incorporating features like personalized recommendations, intelligent search, or automated personalization.

### Staying Competitive

In an increasingly digital world, leveraging AI is key to staying competitive. Businesses that adopt AI technologies can gain significant advantages, from operational efficiencies to enhanced customer insights and experiences.

- **Action Point**: Stay informed about the latest AI developments in your industry. Invest in AI technologies that align with your business goals and customer needs.

Artificial Intelligence represents a transformative power for businesses willing to embrace its potential. By integrating AI into operations, marketing, sales, and innovation efforts, entrepreneurs can significantly enhance efficiency, customer engagement, and competitiveness. As AI technology continues to evolve, staying informed and adaptable will be crucial for leveraging its full potential. The journey into AI for your business is not just about automation and data analysis; it's about reimagining how your business operates and engages with its customers in the digital age.

**Extra Chapter: Behind the Scenes - Writing This Book with Generative AI**

In an era where artificial intelligence (AI) transforms industries, the process of writing and publishing has also undergone a significant evolution. This book, a comprehensive guide for entrepreneurs seeking to build and scale their businesses, harnesses the innovative power of generative AI. This chapter pulls back the curtain, revealing how generative AI played a pivotal role in creating the content, refining ideas, and even influencing the structure of the book itself.

## The Role of Generative AI in Content Creation

Generative AI refers to a subset of artificial intelligence technologies capable of generating new content, from text to images and beyond, based on the data it has been trained on. In the context of writing this book, generative AI was employed to assist with several key tasks:

### Idea Generation and Structuring

One of the initial challenges in any writing project is determining the structure and main topics to cover. Generative AI was utilized to brainstorm ideas for chapters, subtopics, and even case studies by analyzing current trends, common challenges, and opportunities within the entrepreneurial ecosystem.

- **Action Point for Writers**: Leverage AI to generate a content outline. Input your main theme or subject area, and use AI to suggest relevant topics, chapters, and sub-sections that could provide value to your readers.

### Content Drafting

Drafting content can be time-consuming. Generative AI significantly expedited this process by creating initial drafts for sections of the book. These drafts were then reviewed and refined by human editors to ensure accuracy, coherence, and to inject a personal touch that resonates with readers.

- **Action Point for Writers**: Use AI to create first drafts of your content. Set clear parameters for what you need, including tone, length, and key points to cover. Always review and edit AI-generated drafts to ensure they meet your standards.

### Research Assistance

Generative AI tools were invaluable in conducting research for various chapters. By quickly analyzing vast amounts of data, AI provided insights into the latest trends, statistics, and case studies relevant to entrepreneurs today.

- **Action Point for Writers**: Use AI to supplement your research efforts. Input specific research queries to gather preliminary data, statistics, and sources that you can then explore in more depth.

## Enhancing Creativity and Productivity

A common misconception about AI in creative processes is that it might stifle human creativity. On the contrary, our experience showed that AI could act as a catalyst for creativity, suggesting angles and ideas that might not have been immediately apparent. Moreover, by handling routine tasks, AI allowed the human contributors to focus on the creative and strategic aspects of writing.

- **Action Point for Writers**: Approach AI as a creative partner. Allow it to suggest ideas that you can expand upon, refine, or even counter, to spark deeper creativity and innovation in your writing.

## Ethical Considerations and Human Touch

While AI played a significant role in creating this book, ethical considerations and the importance of the human touch were always at the forefront. Ensuring the accuracy of information, maintaining an authentic voice, and upholding ethical standards in AI usage were key priorities.

- **Action Point for Writers**: Always fact-check AI-generated content. Use AI as a tool, not a crutch, and infuse your unique voice and insights to create content that truly resonates with your audience.

The integration of generative AI into the writing process of this book represents a fusion of technology and human creativity, offering a glimpse into the future of content creation. By leveraging AI for idea generation, drafting, and research, the creation of this guide for entrepreneurs was not only streamlined but enriched. This journey underscores the transformative potential of AI in enhancing productivity and creativity, heralding a new era for authors, educators, and creators across industries.

# Sign Off: Embracing the Future Together

As we close the final pages of this guide, it's clear that the journey we've embarked upon together is far from over. The entrepreneurial path is one of constant evolution, learning, and adaptation. In these chapters, we've traversed the landscapes of innovation, strategy, and technology—each step illuminated by the guiding light of ambition and the spirit of perseverance.

This book, conceived in the crucible of generative AI and human collaboration, stands as a testament to what's possible when we harness the power of emerging technologies to amplify our creative and entrepreneurial endeavors. It is my hope that the insights shared herein not only equip you with the knowledge to navigate the complexities of today's business world but also inspire you to envision and create a future brimming with possibilities.

Remember, the essence of entrepreneurship lies not in the certainty of success but in the courage to face the unknown, armed with the conviction that our dreams are worth the pursuit. As you close this book, may you open a new chapter in your entrepreneurial journey with renewed vigor, inspired ideas, and an unwavering commitment to making your mark on the world.

Let this not be a farewell, but an invitation—to innovate, to disrupt, and to lead with purpose. Embrace the challenges ahead, for they are but stepping stones on the path to your greatest achievements. Stay curious, stay driven, and above all, stay true to the vision that set you on this path.

Thank you for allowing me to be a part of your journey. Here's to the ventures yet to be realized, the challenges yet to be overcome, and the successes yet to be celebrated. Together, let's embrace the future, for it is ours to shape.

With warmest regards and best wishes for your continued success,

#Jerremy Specter-Mendam